Brown Bears

Victoria Blakemore

For Loretta, thank you for being such a great team leader

and friend!

© 2018 Victoria Blakemore

vblakemore.author@gmail.com

Copyright info/picture credits

Cover, Relijana/Pixabay; Page 3, Gellinger/Pixabay; Page 5, hmauck/Pixabay; Page 7, Atlantios/Pixabay; Page 9, StockSnap/Pixabay; Pages 10-11, herbert2512/Pixabay; Page 13, Natalia_Kollegova/Pixabay; Page 15, skeeze/Pixabay; Page 17, Alexas_Fotos/Pixabay; Page 19, frank3143/Pixabay; Page 21, skeeze/Pixabay; Page 23; raincarnation40/Pixabay; Page 25, tinella16/AdobeStock; Page 27, skeeze/Pixabay; Page 29, skeeze/Pixabay; Page 31, Natalia_Kollegova/ Pixabay; Page 33, Relijana/Pixabay

Table of Contents

What Are Brown Bears?

Brown bears are large mammals. They are not as large as polar bears, but larger than some black bears.

There are many **variations** of brown bears. They may differ in size, color, and where they live. The grizzly bear is one of the most well-known brown bears.

Brown bears can be many

different shades of brown, from

cream to nearly black.

Size

Brown bears are usually between six and ten feet long. They can be up to four feet tall at the shoulder.

Brown bears can **vary** in weight. Adults can weigh anywhere between 200 and 1,500 pounds.

Male brown bears, or boars,

are larger than female bears,

or sows.

Brown bears have a large, muscular hump on their back. It is especially large in grizzly bears.

They have a very thick coat of fur. It helps to keep them warm in the cold **climate** of their habitat.

Brown bears have very long, sharp

claws. They use their claws for

digging, hunting, and climbing.

Habitat

Brown bears are found in forests and the tundra, which is an area with few trees and plants.

They live in areas where it can get very cold. Many brown bears are found close to a river or stream, where they can catch fish.

Range

Brown bears are found on the continents of North America, Europe, and Asia.

Many are found in Russia, Alaska, Canada, Norway, and California.

Diet

Brown bears are **omnivores**.
They eat both meat and
plants.

Their diet is made up of small
animals, fish, insects, fruits,
grass, roots, and plant bulbs.
They also eat leftover prey
from other animals.

In places like Alaska and Russia, brown bears eat a lot of salmon. They hunt for salmon as the fish swim in rivers and streams.

Brown bears are very helpful to their habitats. When they are digging for food, they are stirring the soil. This releases **nitrogen** and keeps the soil good for plants.

They also help to spread seeds. The seeds from the fruit they eat are spread through their **waste**.

The largest male bears, get to

choose where they will do

their fishing first.

Communication

Brown bears use scent, sound, and movement to communicate with each other.

They have a scent they can use to mark their **territory**. They also use sounds like growls, grunts, and blowing out air. They do not use sound as often as scent or movement.

Bears may play fight or wrestle

when they are young. As they

get older, the fights are not for

playing. They show **aggression**. 17

Movement

Brown bears are very fast for animals of their large size. They can run at speeds of up to thirty miles per hour.

Although brown bears can climb, they are not as good at climbing as other kinds of bears.

Brown bears typically don't run

unless they are chasing prey,

defending their cubs, or on the

attack.

Brown Bear Cubs

Brown bears usually have a **litter** of two cubs. They are born almost hairless, without teeth, and with their eyes shut.

Cubs are born in the winter. The mother has plenty of fat stored up for the winter. She is able to provide her cubs with food.

Cubs stay with their mother for between two and six years. She teaches them how to find food and keeps them safe from predators.

Brown Bear Life

Brown bears are usually **solitary**. They spend most of their time alone. The main exception to this is a mother and her cubs.

They are mainly **diurnal**, which means that they are most active during the day. In some areas, they may be more active at night.

When they are not looking for

food, brown bears are often

seen resting.

Hibernating

Although brown bears do sleep through the winter, it is not true **hibernation**. It is something called **torpor**.

Torpor is a deep sleep where an animal saves energy and lives off its fat stores. The bear's **metabolism** slows down when in torpor.

Brown bears make their den in

the side of a hill, under the brush,

in a tree hollow, or in a cave.

Population

In the year 2017, there were thought to be around 200,000 brown bears left in the wild. They are not currently **endangered.**

Although there are many left, their habitats are much smaller than they used to be. This is a growing problem for bears.

In the wild, brown bears live

about twenty-five years. They

often live longer in zoos.

Brown Bears in Danger

Habitat destruction is a big problem for brown bears. Their habitats are being destroyed for logging, farming, mining, and building.

Brown bears are coming into more contact with humans. This is dangerous for humans and the bears.

Brown bears are coming closer

to places where people live to

try to find food to eat.

Helping Brown Bears

Many groups are trying to help brown bears. They are doing this in several ways. One way is by setting aside protected land. This provides the bears with a safe habitat.

Groups are also working to prevent brown bears from being hunted.

In some places, special fences are being built around farms and areas with **livestock**. This is to protect them from brown bears. It also protects the brown bears from coming into contact with humans.

The goal of these groups is to keep brown bears alive and safe in the wild.

Glossary

Aggression: showing that you are mean, unfriendly, ready to fight

Climate: the weather in a certain place

Diurnal: an animal that is most active during the day

Endangered: at risk of becoming extinct

Hibernation: when an animal sleeps through the winter to save energy

Litter: animals born at the same time

Livestock: animals that are kept on farms

Metabolism: the process of changing food into energy

Nitrogen: an element found in living things

Omnivore: an animal that eats meat and plants

Solitary: living alone

Territory: an area of land that an animal clams as its own

Torpor: when an animal is dormant, or sleeping for long periods of time

Variation: a different form or version of something

Vary: to change

Waste: material given off by the body after food is digested

About the Author

Victoria Blakemore is a first grade

teacher in Southwest Florida with a

passion for reading.

You can visit her at

www.elementaryexplorers.com

Also in This Series

Gray Wolves	Sloths	Flamingos	Camels	Koalas	Honey Bees	Pandas
Pangolins	White-Tailed Deer	Orcas	Giraffes	Corn	Meerkats	Echidnas
Walruses	Raccoons	Bald Eagles	Apples	Arctic Foxes	Red Pandas	Cassowaries
Tigers	Ladybugs	Moose	Beluga Whales	Leopards	Elephants	Jellyfish
Binturongs	Lions	Dolphins	Reindeer	Hammerhead Sharks	Hippos	Pumpkins
Peafowl	Chameleons	Florida Panthers	Aye-Ayes	Black Bears	Cheetahs	Manatees
Gingerbread	Polar Bears	Hot Chocolate	Orangutans	Coyotes	Marshmallows	Strawberries

Victoria Blakemore

Also in This Series

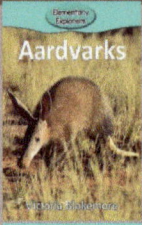

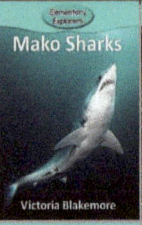

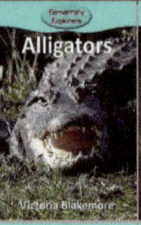

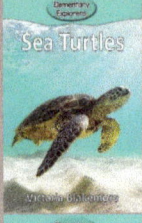

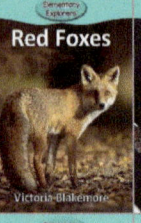

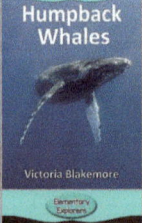

Aardvarks	Mako Sharks	Alligators	Frogs	Hedgehogs	Brown Bears	Bongos
Sea Turtles	Quokkas	Muskrats	Zebras	Red Foxes	Ring-Tailed Lemurs	Platypuses
Anteaters	Kangaroos	Rhinos	Jaguars	Wombats	Capybaras	Gorillas
Cats	Skunks	Butterflies	Dingoes	Snow Leopards	African Wild Dogs	Penguins
Whale Sharks	Wolverines	Warthogs	Caracals	Badgers	Seals	Hummingbirds
Pikas	Humpback Whales	Pumas	Lemonade	Llamas	Tulips	Ostriches
Sunflowers	Fennec Foxes	Sea Lions	Squirrels	Roses	Porcupines	Ice Cream

Elementary Explorers

Victoria Blakemore

www.ingramcontent.com/pod-product-compliance
Lightning Source LLC
Chambersburg PA
CBHW051250020426
42333CB00025B/3150

9 781947 439900